W9-CJO-401

Ecuador

by Joyce Markovics

Consultant: Karla Ruiz
Teacher's College, Columbia University
New York, New York

PUBLISHING

New York, New York

Credits

Cover, © GlobalStock/iStock and Elena Kalistratova/iStock; 3, © Smileus/Shutterstock; 4, © Jess Kraft/Shutterstock; 5L, © Steffen Foerster/Shutterstock; 5R, © Villamilk/iStock; 6, © Javarman/Dreamstime; 7, © Jess Kraft/Dreamstime; 8, © Ksenia Ragozina/Shutterstock; 9, © Ecuadorpostales/Shutterstock; 10, © Sheila Say/Shutterstock; 11T, © Fotos593/Shutterstock; 11B, © tamara bizjak/Shutterstock; 12, © Sean Pavone/Shutterstock; 13, © PRISMA ARCHIVO/Alamy Stock Photo; 14–15, © Jess Kraft/Shutterstock; 15, © Mcwilli1/Dreamstime; 16, © FrankvandenBergh/iStock; 17, © Ksenia Ragozina/Shutterstock; 18, © bonga1965/Shutterstock; 19T, © loops7/iStock; 19BL, © zirconicusso/Shutterstock; 19BR, © dextorTh/iStock; 20, © Pierre Jean Duriew/Dreamstime; 21, © Steffen Foerster/Dreamstime; 22, © Maxisport/Shutterstock; 23, © AGIF/Shutterstock; 24T, © val lawless/Shutterstock; 24B, © Pablo Hidalgo/Dreamstime; 25, © Aleksander Mirski/iStock; 26T, © Roberto Orrú/Alamy Stock Photo; 26B, © Ildi Papp/Shutterstock; 27, © Ildi Papp/Shutterstock; 28L, © ILYA AKINSHIN/Shutterstock; 28–29, © Pablo Hidalgo/Dreamstime; 30T, © imagestock/iStock; 30B, © johnbraid/Shutterstock; 31(T to B), © Fotos593/Shutterstock, © mr_wilke/iStock, © pxhidalgo/iStock, © Villamilk/iStock, © stockcam/iStock, and © shalamov/iStock; 32, © Lenor Ko/Shutterstock.

Publisher: Kenn Goin
Senior Editor: Joyce Tavolacci
Creative Director: Spencer Brinker
Design: Debrah Kaiser
Photo Researcher: Olympia Shannon

Library of Congress Cataloging-in-Publication Data

Names: Markovics, Joyce L., author.
Title: Ecuador / by Joyce Markovics.
Description: New York, New York : Bearport Publishing, [2017] | Series:
   Countries we come from | Includes bibliographical references and index. |
   Audience: Ages 6–10._
Identifiers: LCCN 2016006800 (print) | LCCN 2016007077 (ebook) | ISBN
   9781944102715 (library binding) | ISBN 9781944102883 (ebook)
Subjects: LCSH: Ecuador—Juvenile literature.
Classification: LCC F3708.5 .M37 2017 (print) | LCC F3708.5 (ebook) | DDC
   986.6—dc23
LC record available at http://lccn.loc.gov/2016006800

For more information, write to Bearport Publishing Company, Inc., 45 West 21st Street, Suite 3B, New York, New York 10010. Printed in the United States of America.

10 9 8 7 6 5 4 3 2 1

Contents

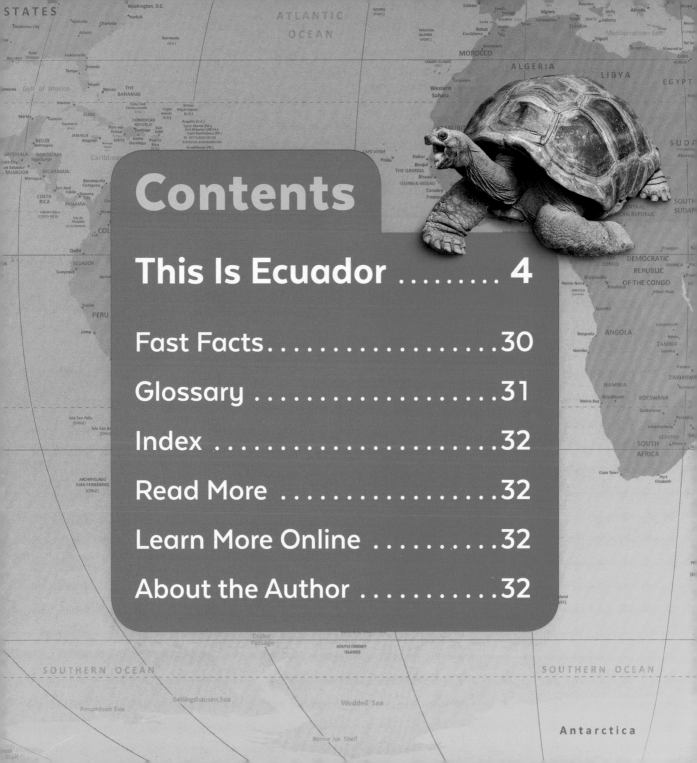

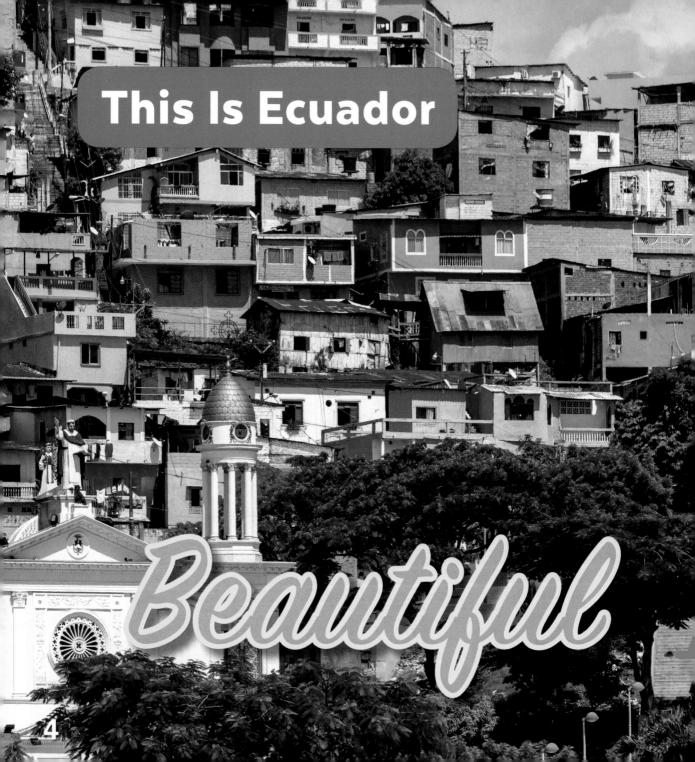

This Is Ecuador

Beautiful

WILD

FULL OF WONDER

5

Ecuador is one of the smallest countries in South America.

Yet more than 16 million people live there.

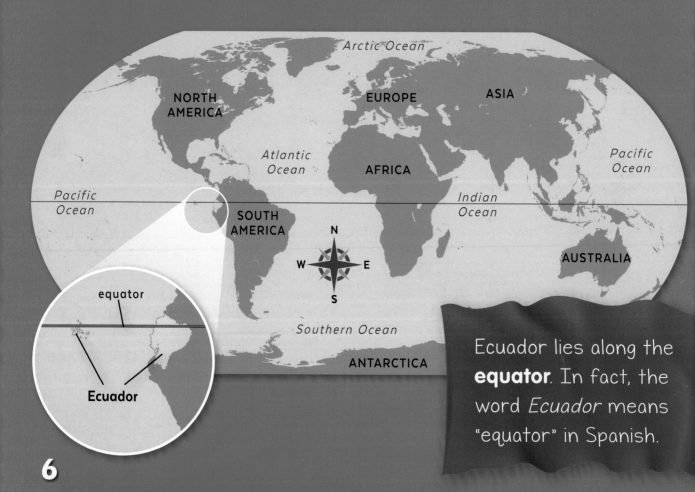

Arctic Ocean

NORTH AMERICA

EUROPE

ASIA

Atlantic Ocean

AFRICA

Pacific Ocean

Pacific Ocean

SOUTH AMERICA

Indian Ocean

N

W   E

S

AUSTRALIA

Southern Ocean

ANTARCTICA

equator

Ecuador

Ecuador lies along the **equator**. In fact, the word *Ecuador* means "equator" in Spanish.

The country has jungles, plains, and mountains.

8

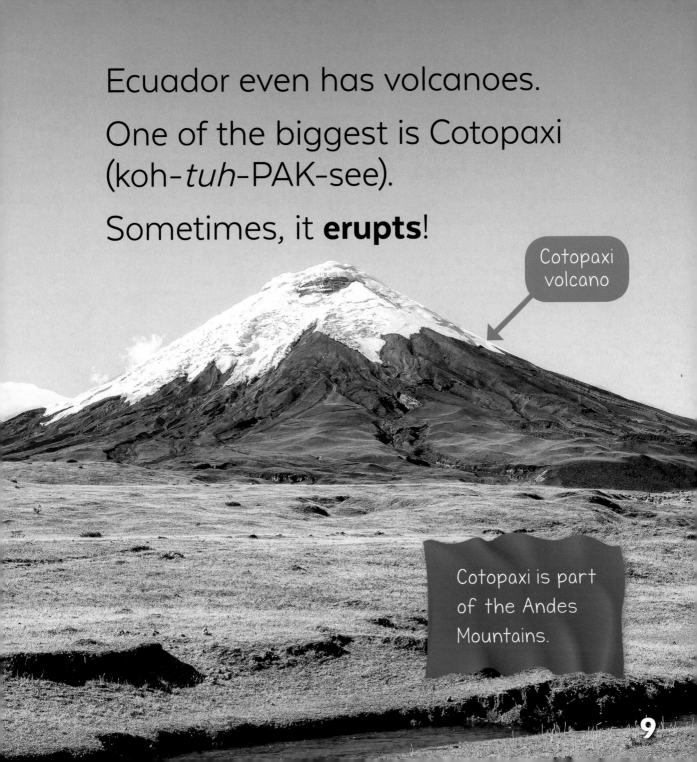

Ecuador even has volcanoes.

One of the biggest is Cotopaxi (koh-*tuh*-PAK-see).

Sometimes, it **erupts**!

Cotopaxi volcano

Cotopaxi is part of the Andes Mountains.

The Galápagos Islands are part of Ecuador.

They are home to **unique** creatures.

Many **tourists** visit the islands each year.

Tortoises there can weigh 500 pounds (227 kg).

Galápagos tortoise

Strange seabirds have blue feet!

blue-footed boobies

People have lived in Ecuador for thousands of years.

The Inca were one of the earliest groups to settle there.

The Inca once ruled much of South America.

Clay objects made by the Inca people

In the 1500s, Spain fought the Inca and won control of Ecuador.

Then Ecuador became a free country in 1822.

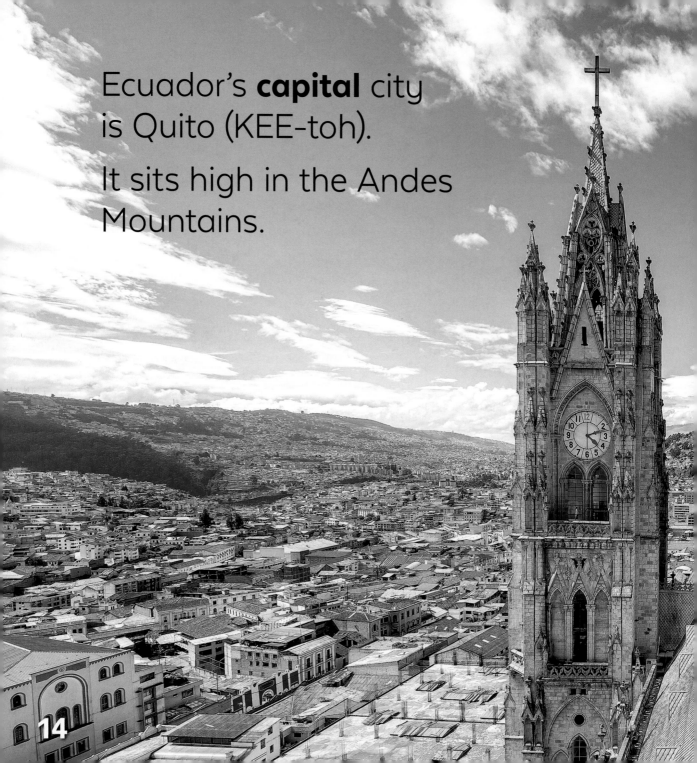

Ecuador's **capital** city is Quito (KEE-toh).

It sits high in the Andes Mountains.

Quito is the second-highest capital city in the world!

More than 1.5 million people live and work in Quito.

The largest city in Ecuador is Guayaquil (WHY-ah-kil).

More than two million people live there.

Large lizards make their homes in the city's parks.

These scaly animals are iguanas (ih-GWAH-*nuhs*).

Iguanas can grow 5 feet (1.5 m) long!

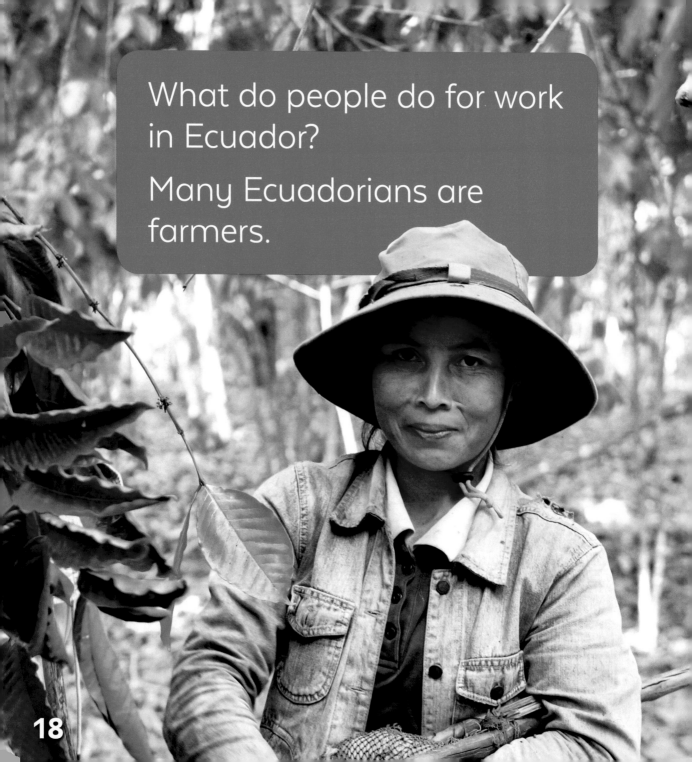

What do people do for work in Ecuador?

Many Ecuadorians are farmers.

18

They grow bananas, rice, and coffee beans.

Most of the world's bananas are grown in Ecuador.

rice

coffee beans

Most Ecuadorians speak Spanish.

This is how you say *good* in Spanish:

Bueno (BWAY-noh)

This is how you say *bad*:

Malo (MAH-loh)

Some people speak a **native** language called Quechua (KEESH–wah). *Ari* (ah–REE) means "yes" in Quechua.

21

For fun, many Ecuadorians play sports.

They especially love soccer.

Soccer is called *fútbol* (FOOT–bohl) in Ecuador.

Go team, go!

Ecuador has many festivals.

In November, people celebrate the Day of the Dead.

Ecuadorians make special bread for the Day of the Dead. It's shaped like a person!

On this day, loved ones who have died are remembered.

What do Ecuadorians like to eat?

Rice, fried bananas, and meats are popular.

Ecuadorians also eat *cuy* (KOO–ee). Cuy is roasted guinea pig!

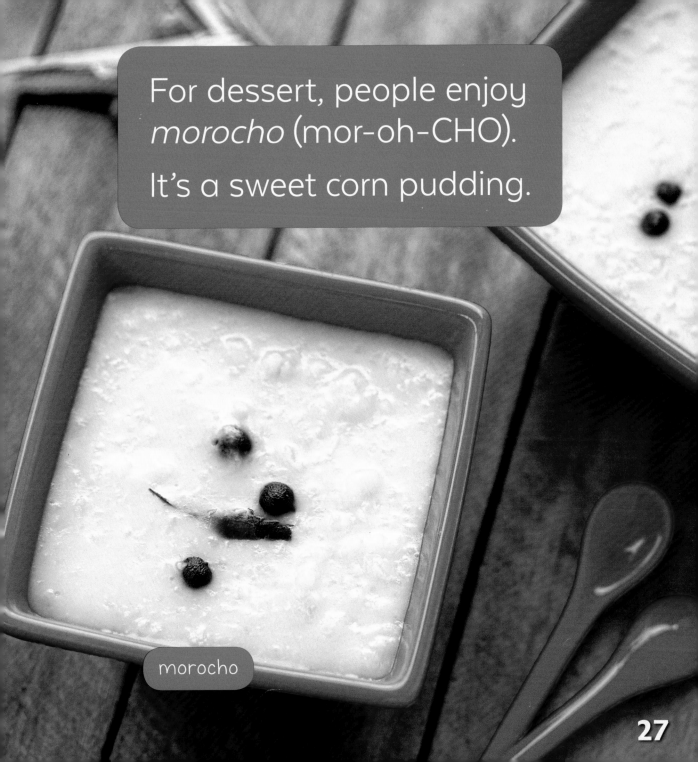

For dessert, people enjoy *morocho* (mor-oh-CHO).

It's a sweet corn pudding.

morocho

27

Ecuadorians love *pasillo* (pah-SEE-oh) music.

It's often played with a guitar and flute.

This music can be heard throughout Ecuador!

Ecuadorians also enjoy dancing to pasillo music.

Fast Facts

Capital city: Quito

Population of Ecuador: More than 16 million

Main languages: Spanish and Quechua

Money: U.S. dollar

Major religion: Roman Catholic

Neighboring countries: Colombia and Peru

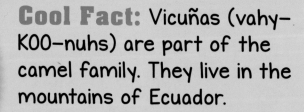

Cool Fact: Vicuñas (vahy-KOO-nuhs) are part of the camel family. They live in the mountains of Ecuador.

capital (KAP-uh-tuhl) a city where a country's government is based

equator (i-KWAY-tur) the imaginary line around the middle of the Earth

erupts (i-RUPTS) to send out lava, ash, steam, and gas from a volcano

native (NAY-tiv) belonging to a particular place

tourists (TOOR-ists) people who travel and visit places for fun

unique (yoo-NEEK) one of a kind; like no other

Index

Read More

Owings, Lisa. *Ecuador (Exploring Countries).* Minneapolis, MN: Bellwether Media (2015).

Williams, Colleen Madonna Flood. *Ecuador (South America Today).* Broomall, PA: Mason Crest (2009).

Learn More Online

To learn more about Ecuador, visit
www.bearportpublishing.com/CountriesWeComeFrom

About the Author

Joyce Markovics lives in a very old house along the Hudson River. She dreams of visiting the Galápagos Islands.